C0-DXA-526

Now I Know the 10 Commandments

I THOU SHALT HAVE NO OTHER GODS BEFORE ME
II THOU SHALT NOT MAKE UNTO THEE ANY GRAVEN IMAGE
III THOU SHALT NOT TAKE THE NAME OF THE LORD THY GOD IN VAIN
IV REMEMBER THE SABBATH DAY TO KEEP IT HOLY
V HONOUR THY FATHER AND THY MOTHER

VI THOU SHALT NOT KILL
VII THOU SHALT NOT COMMIT ADULTERY
VIII THOU SHALT NOT STEAL
IX THOU SHALT NOT BEAR FALSE WITNESS AGAINST THY NEIGHBOUR
X THOU SHALT NOT COVET

Written by Jan Allen

Illustrations by Russ Allen

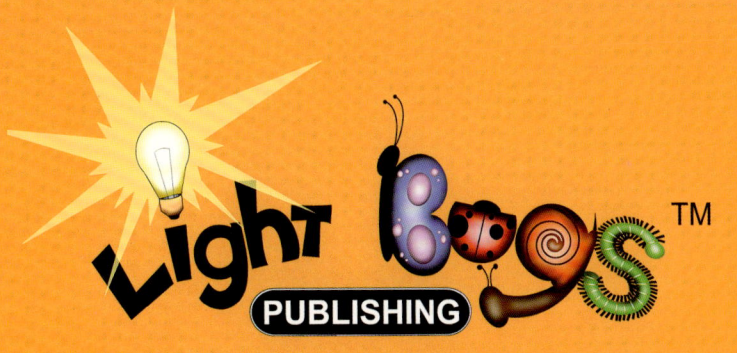

Light Bugs Publishing™

www.lightbugspublishing.com

NOW I KNOW THE TEN COMMANDMENTS

© 2005 Russ Allen

All rights reserved. No portion of this book may be reproduced, stored in a retrieval system, or transmitted in any form or by any means—electronic, mechanical, photocopy, recording, or any other—except for brief quotation in printed reviews, without the prior permission of the publisher.

Published by Light Bugs Publishing, 3749 D. Gulf Breeze Parkway, Suite 336, Gulf Breeze, Florida 32563.
Printed in China.

All Scripture quotations are taken from The King James Version of the Bible (KJV).

Edited by Lori Jones.

Library of Congress Control Number: 2005900346

ISBN: 0-9765514-0-3

This book is dedicated to…

My Lord and Savior, Jesus Christ
My parents, Dennis and Jan Allen
My little sister, Elizabeth
Jaime Scott
Reverend Stan Lewis
and
Larry Mott

Hey there, my name is Sally and this is my totally awesome book about...

God's Ten Commandments!!!

You see, I've thought up this great, new way to remember all Ten Commandments. It's really easy and really fun. I can't wait for you to check it out. So, c'mon, turn the page!

I
THOU SHALT HAVE
NO OTHER GODS BEFORE ME
II
THOU SHALT NOT MAKE
UNTO THEE
ANY GRAVEN IMAGE
III
THOU SHALT NOT TAKE
THE NAME OF
THE LORD THY GOD IN VAIN
IV
REMEMBER THE SABBATH DAY
TO KEEP IT HOLY
V
HONOUR THY FATHER
AND THY MOTHER

Did you know that God wrote the Ten Commandments on two big stones a waaaaaaay long time ago? You'd think ten things would be easy to remember, but people still have a hard time after all these years. So one day I was thinking (I do that a lot) and BING! I had it. It's easier to remember pictures than words, right?

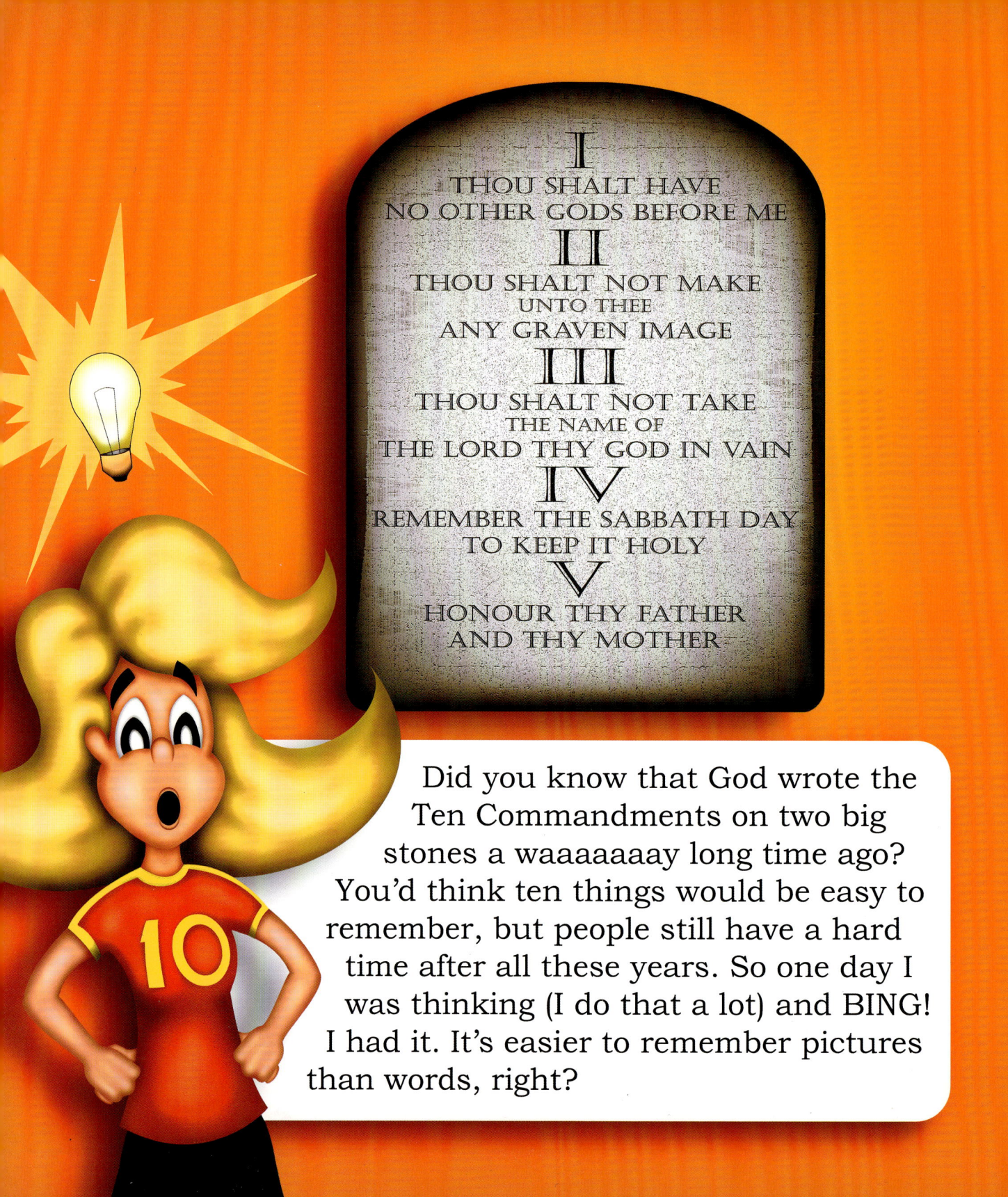

VI
THOU SHALT NOT KILL

VII
THOU SHALT NOT COMMIT ADULTERY

VIII
THOU SHALT NOT STEAL

IX
THOU SHALT NOT BEAR FALSE WITNESS AGAINST THY NEIGHBOUR

X
THOU SHALT NOT COVET

That's when I decided to make a picture for each commandment. And, I hid the commandment's number inside the picture. Pretty clever, huh? So Commandment One has a 1 hiding in its picture. Commandment Two has a 2 hiding and so on and so on—all the way through ten. Ready to find the numbers? Great! Let's begin.

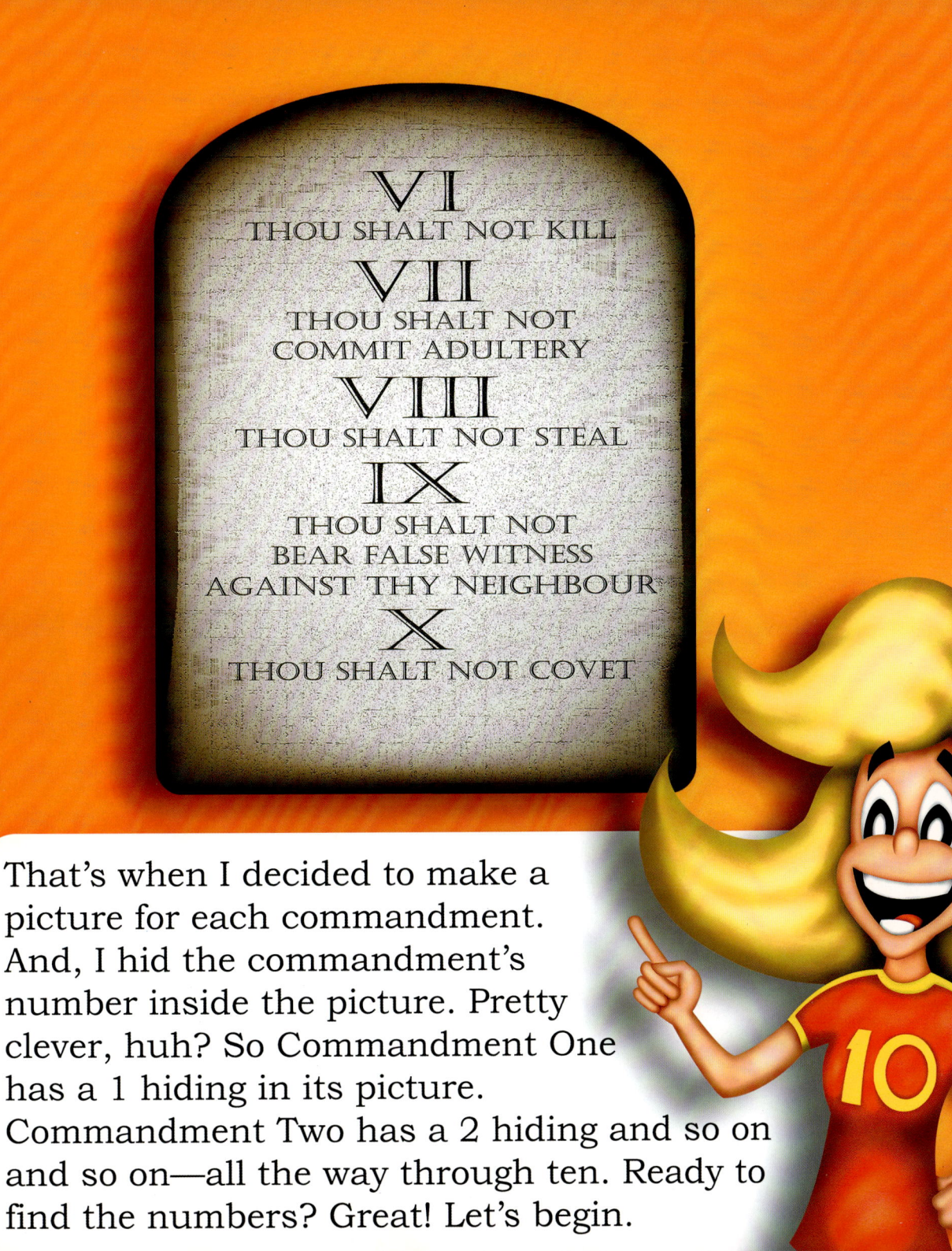

My first commandment picture is Jesus on the cross. That's His mother, Mary, crying. It makes me sad, too, when I see Jesus there.

The cross reminds me of Commandment One because when you draw a cross, the first thing you draw is a one. The commandment says there is only one God and no others—just one true God.

Have you found the 1 yet? Need a hint? Look closely at the cross.

Thou shalt have no other gods before Me.
Exodus 20:3

Can you find the number 1?

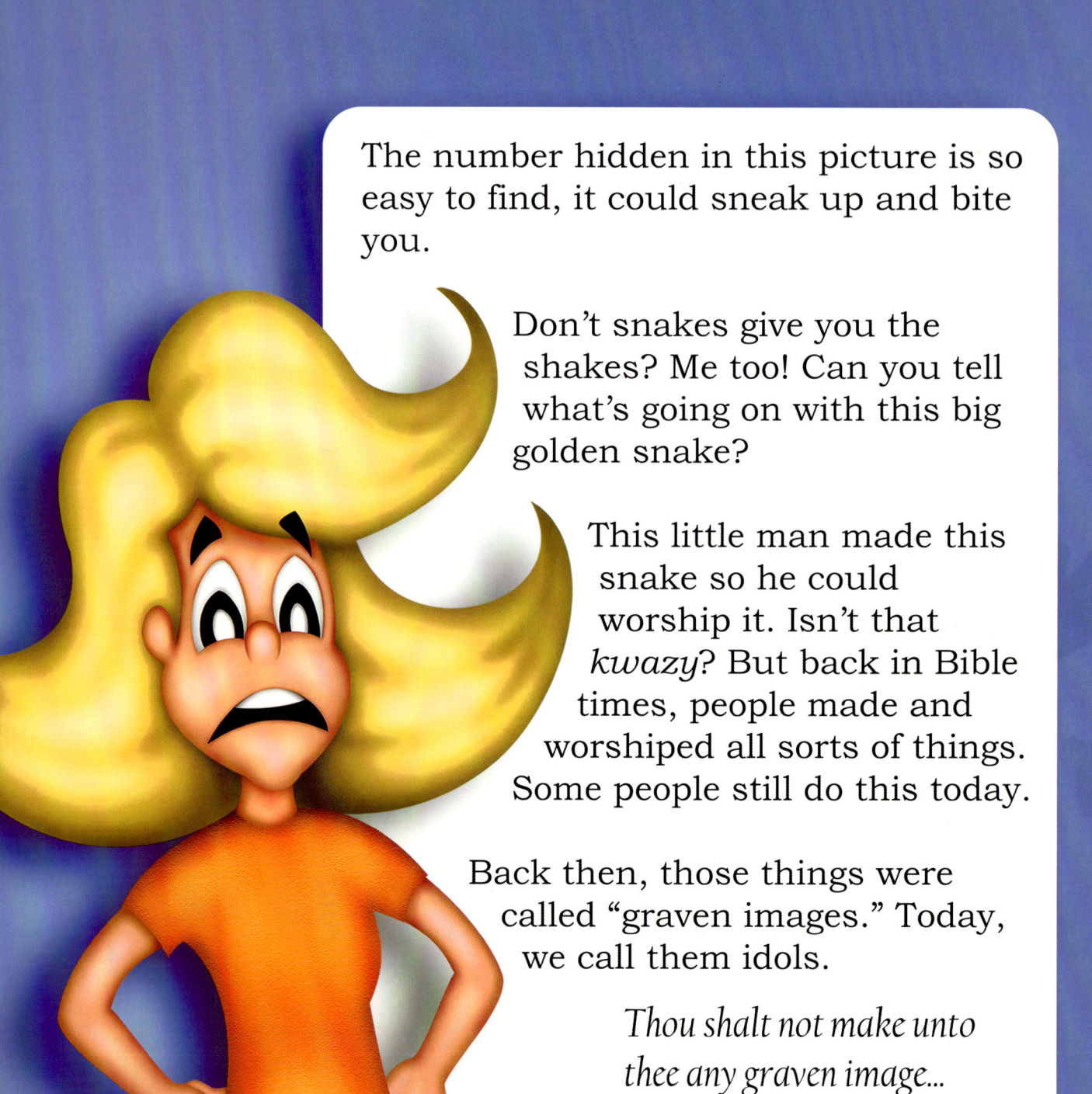

The number hidden in this picture is so easy to find, it could sneak up and bite you.

Don't snakes give you the shakes? Me too! Can you tell what's going on with this big golden snake?

This little man made this snake so he could worship it. Isn't that *kwazy*? But back in Bible times, people made and worshiped all sorts of things. Some people still do this today.

Back then, those things were called "graven images." Today, we call them idols.

Thou shalt not make unto thee any graven image...
Exodus 20:4

Can you find the number ②?

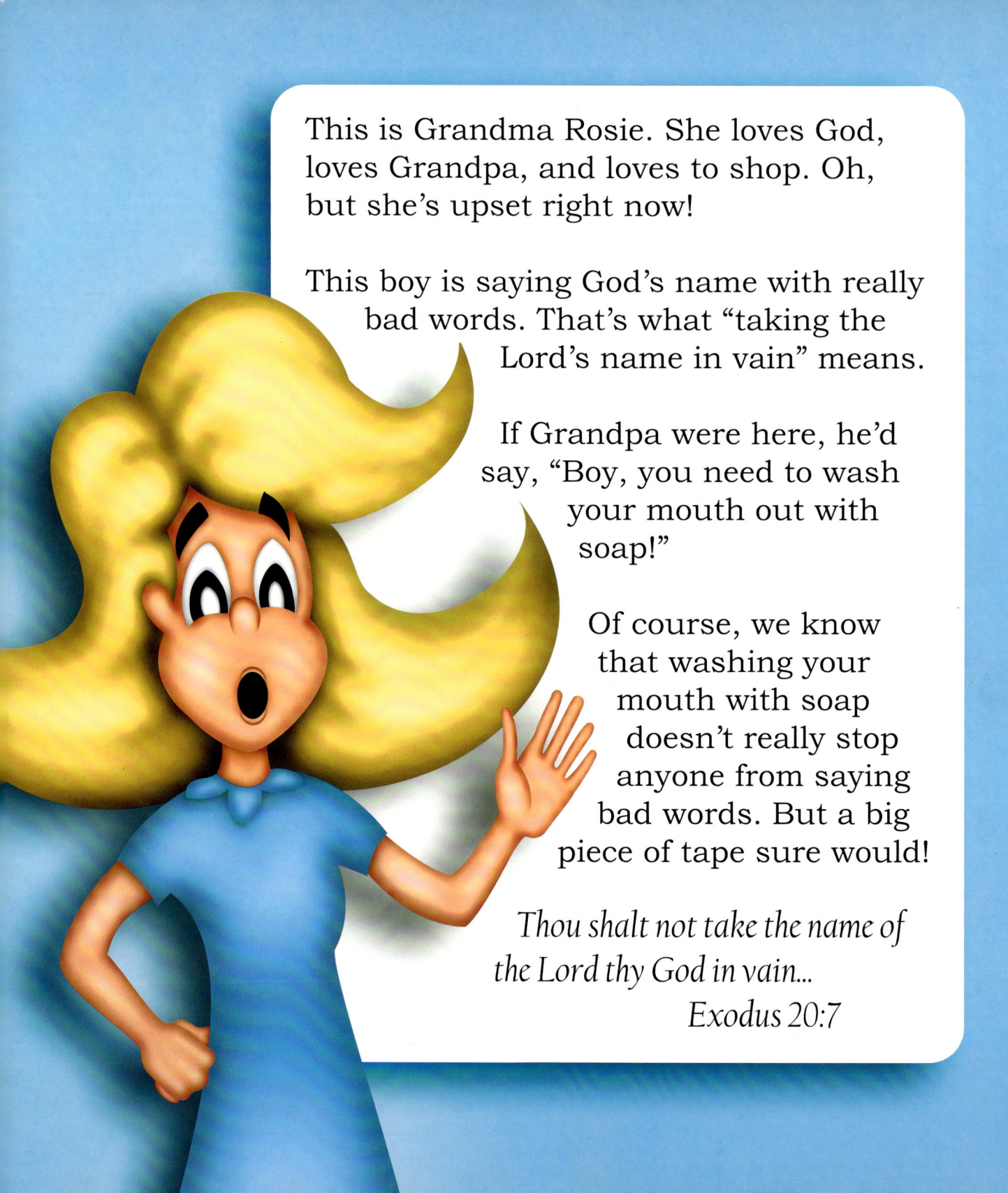

This is Grandma Rosie. She loves God, loves Grandpa, and loves to shop. Oh, but she's upset right now!

This boy is saying God's name with really bad words. That's what "taking the Lord's name in vain" means.

If Grandpa were here, he'd say, "Boy, you need to wash your mouth out with soap!"

Of course, we know that washing your mouth with soap doesn't really stop anyone from saying bad words. But a big piece of tape sure would!

Thou shalt not take the name of the Lord thy God in vain...
Exodus 20:7

Can you find the number 3?

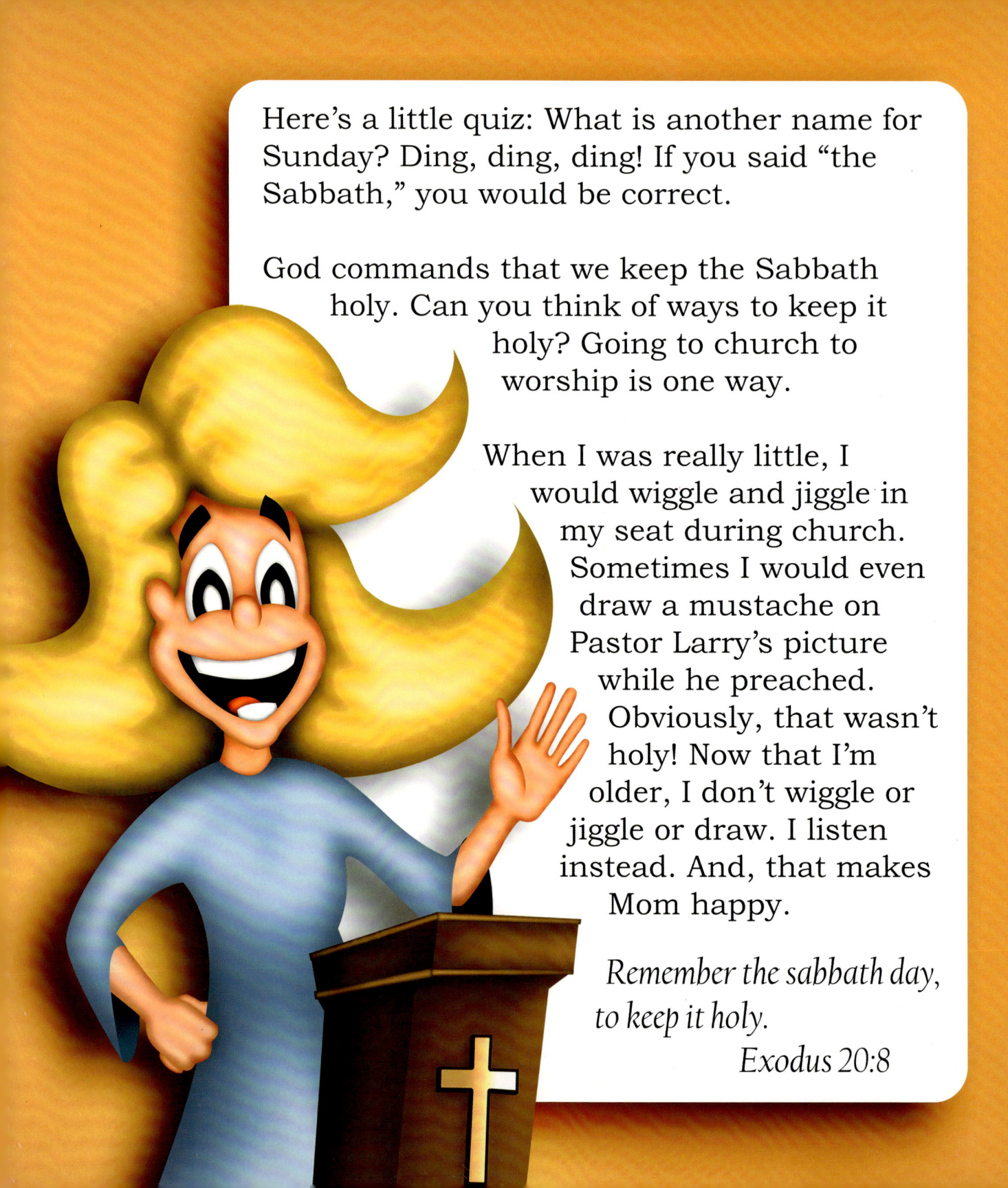

Here's a little quiz: What is another name for Sunday? Ding, ding, ding! If you said "the Sabbath," you would be correct.

God commands that we keep the Sabbath holy. Can you think of ways to keep it holy? Going to church to worship is one way.

When I was really little, I would wiggle and jiggle in my seat during church. Sometimes I would even draw a mustache on Pastor Larry's picture while he preached. Obviously, that wasn't holy! Now that I'm older, I don't wiggle or jiggle or draw. I listen instead. And, that makes Mom happy.

Remember the sabbath day, to keep it holy.

Exodus 20:8

Can you find the number 4?

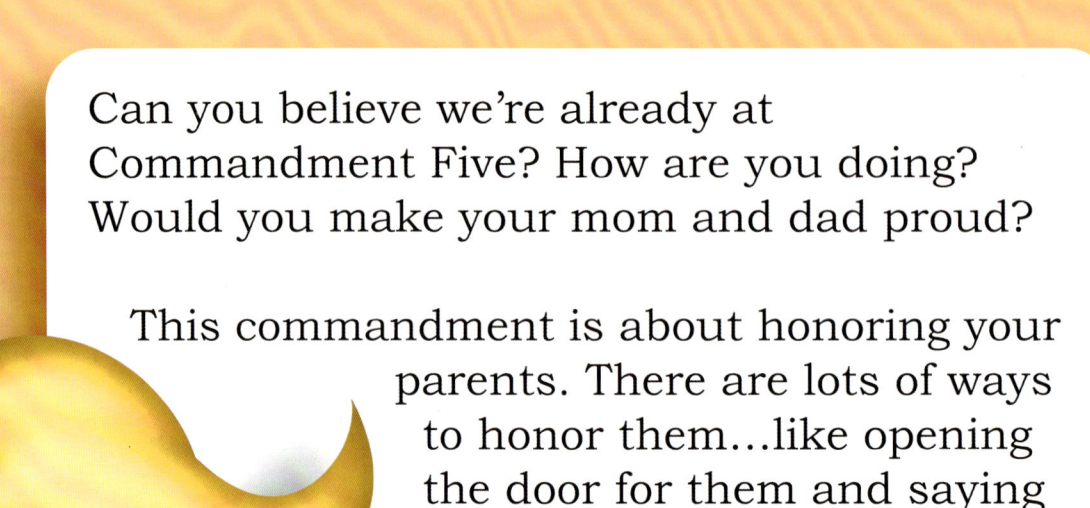

Can you believe we're already at Commandment Five? How are you doing? Would you make your mom and dad proud?

This commandment is about honoring your parents. There are lots of ways to honor them…like opening the door for them and saying "yes, ma'am" and "yes, sir."

What other ways can you think of to honor your parents? What about cleaning your room? Or being nice to your brother or sister?

Honour thy father and thy mother…
Exodus 20:12

Can you find the number 5?

Can you guess this commandment? It's pretty easy if I say so myself.

Could it be...Thou shalt not shoot? Thou shalt not hang? Thou shalt not plant a cactus in the desert?

No! It's "Thou shalt not kill."

Aren't you glad you didn't live in the old cowboy days? They didn't pay too much attention to laws. I suspect they would just shoot and scoot!

Thou shalt not kill.
Exodus 20:13

Can you find the number 6?

What do you think is wrong with this picture? The man walking with his wife can't stop looking at that other woman!

God says when we get married, we are supposed to love only the person we marry. HELLO? That means "Don't be checking out the woman in the purple veil!"

Ready for the next commandment? We're up to number 8.

Thou shalt not commit adultery.
Exodus 20:14

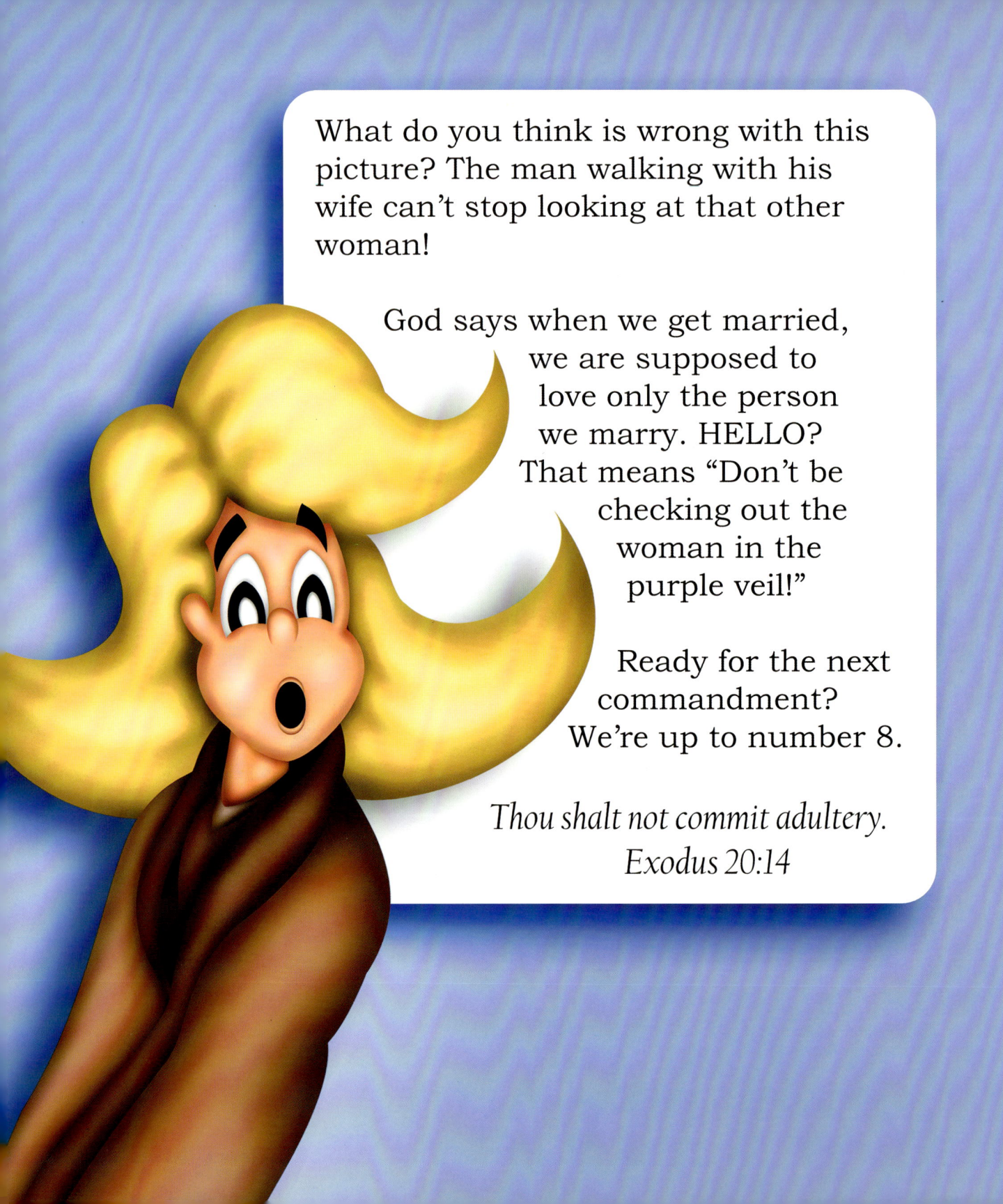

Can you find the number 7?

Burglar, bandit, thief…they all mean the same thing—someone who steals from others. And of course, God says that's something we shouldn't do.

Do you think this thief is coming or going? Either way, he's busted and headed for the big house. The policeman is there with new bracelets to go with this thief's beautiful, blue burglar outfit.

(Here's a secret: "Bracelets" is a police word for handcuffs.)

Thou shalt not steal.
Exodus 20:15

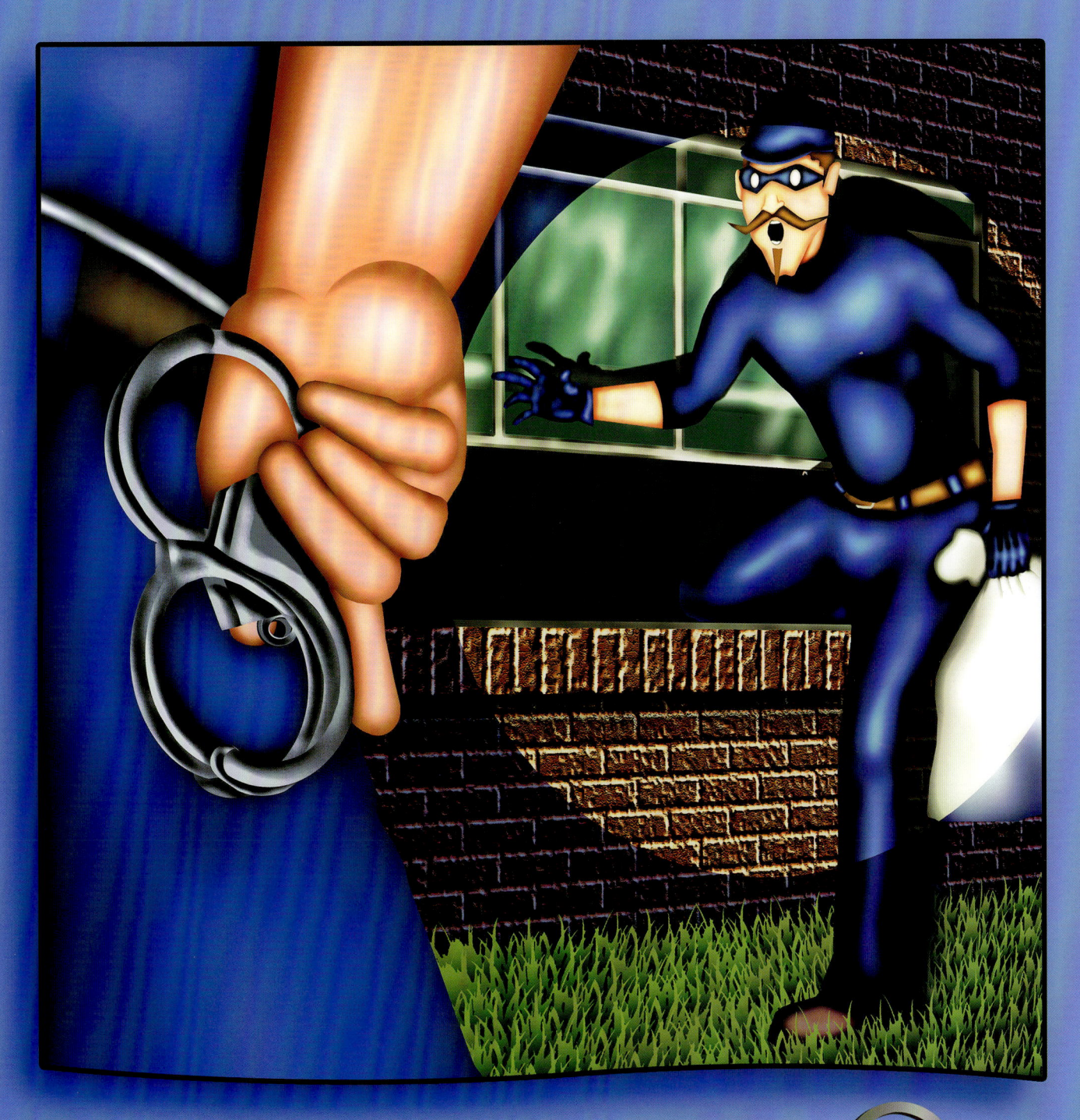

Can you find the number 8?

Lying! That's what this commandment is all about. In the Bible, they call it "bearing false witness."

Has someone ever told you a lie? How did that make you feel? Not so good, right? That's why we should always tell the truth.

And, what about this? "Liar, liar, pants on fire!" Can someone pleeeeease tell me what that means?

Thou shalt not bear false witness against thy neighbour.
Exodus 20:16

Can you find the number 9?

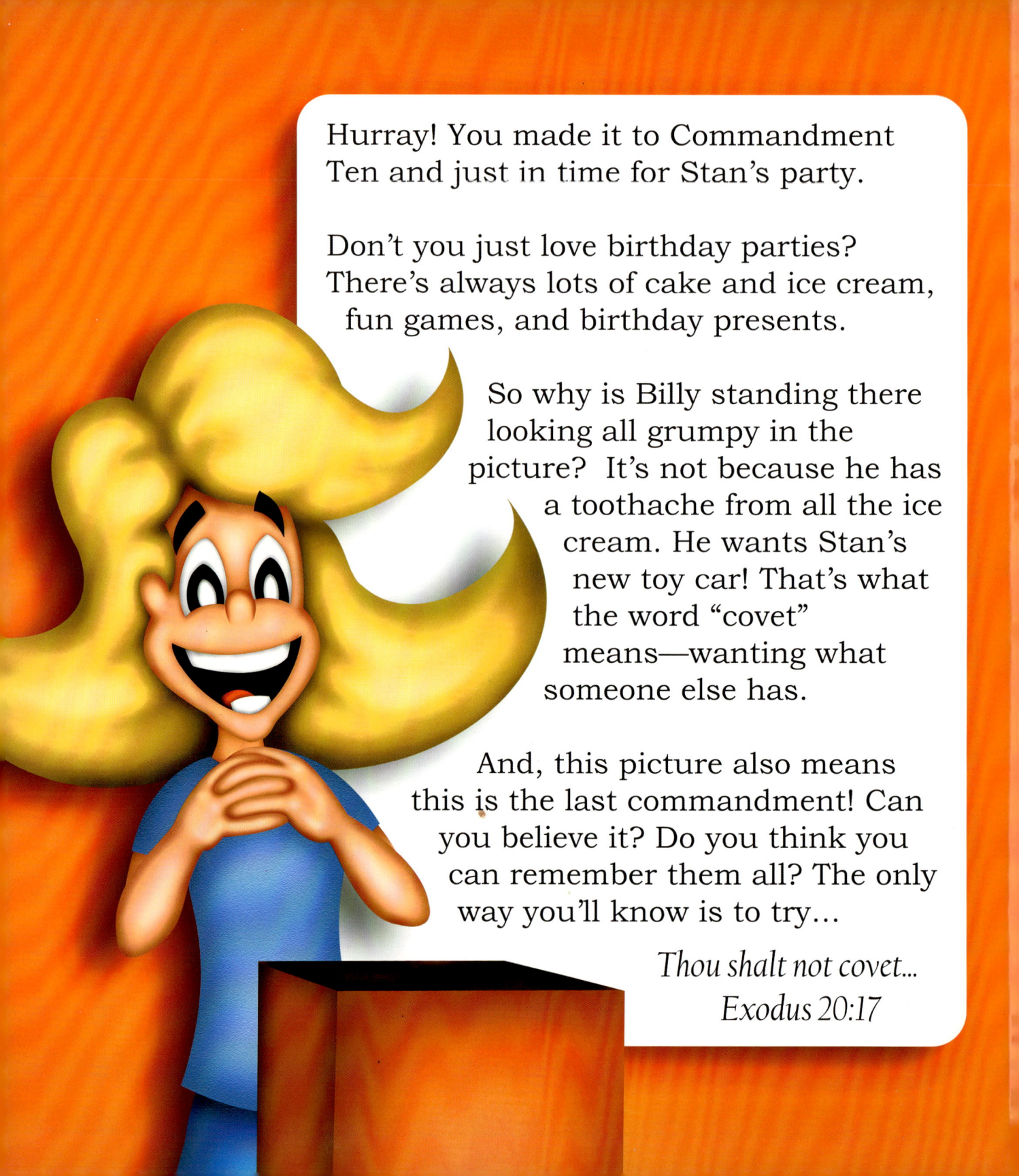

Hurray! You made it to Commandment Ten and just in time for Stan's party.

Don't you just love birthday parties? There's always lots of cake and ice cream, fun games, and birthday presents.

So why is Billy standing there looking all grumpy in the picture? It's not because he has a toothache from all the ice cream. He wants Stan's new toy car! That's what the word "covet" means—wanting what someone else has.

And, this picture also means this is the last commandment! Can you believe it? Do you think you can remember them all? The only way you'll know is to try...

Thou shalt not covet...
Exodus 20:17

Can you find the number 10?

Need a little review? To speed things up, I've put all ten hidden numbers on one page. Remember the cowboy's rope or the policeman's handcuffs? Remember the cross? They're all here.

You've done it! Great job! And now you know the Ten Commandments!

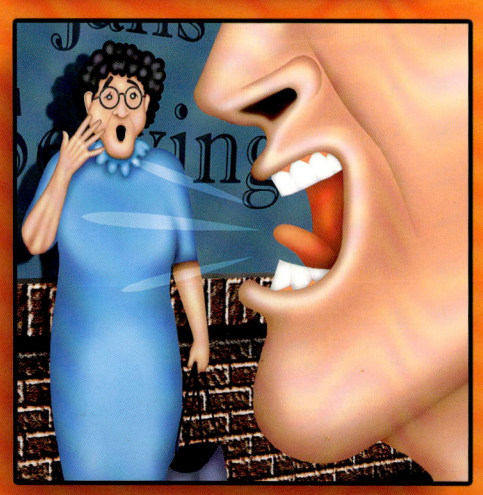

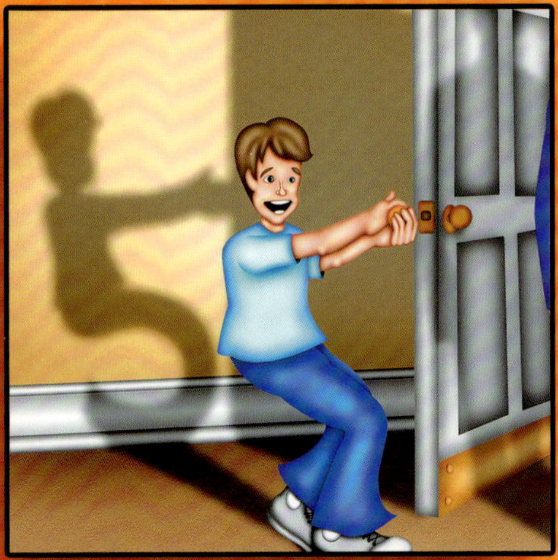
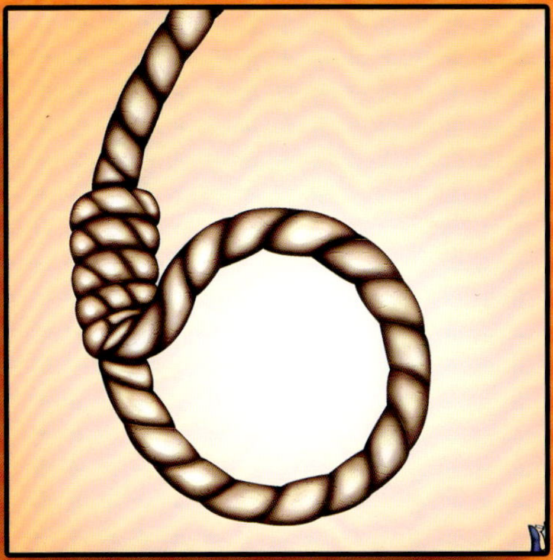
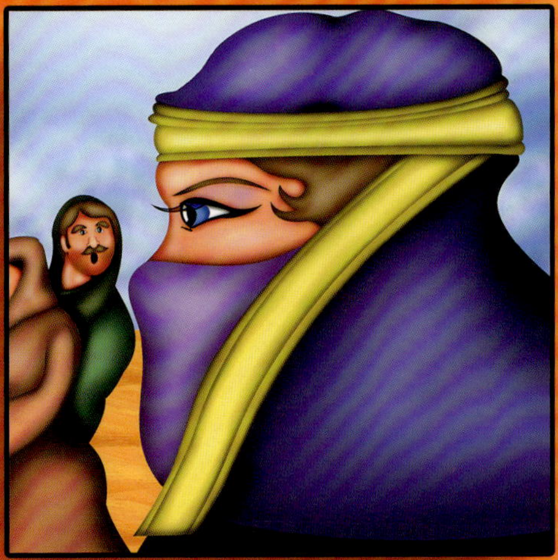
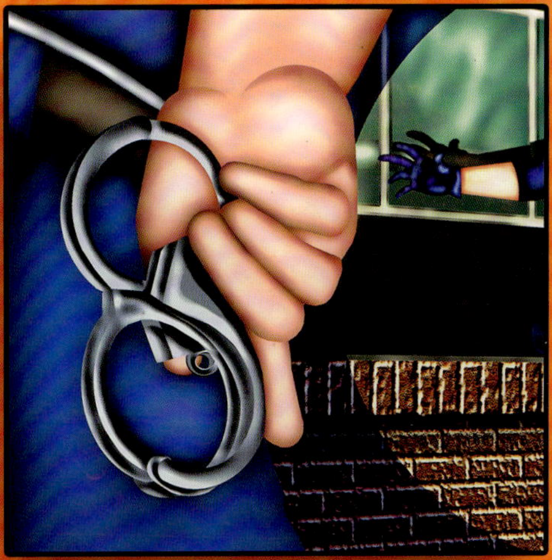
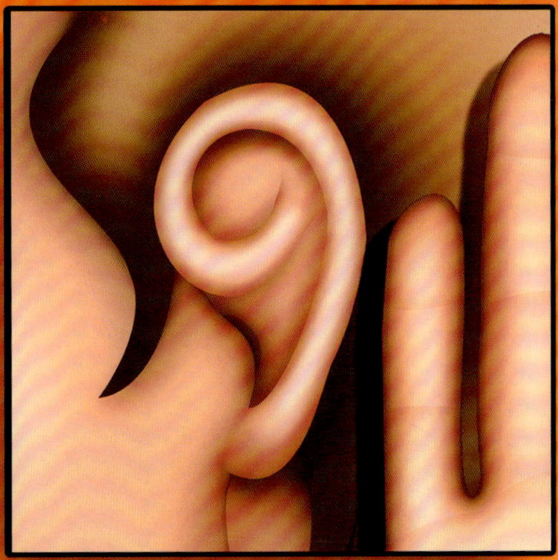
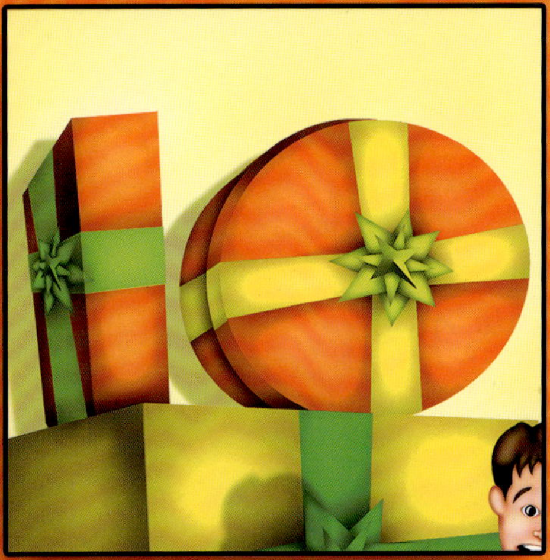

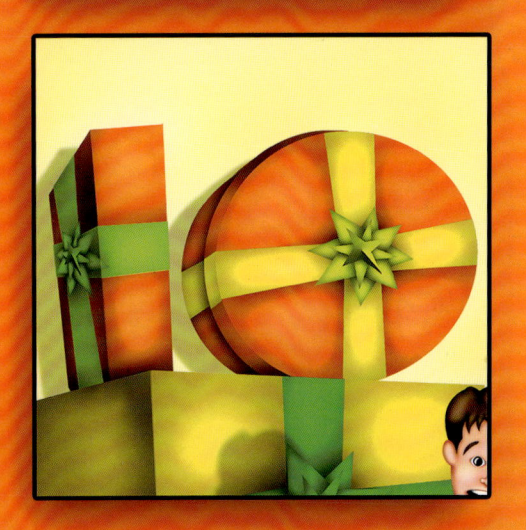

Stop! Wait! Don't close the book yet! I have one more thing to tell you. And it's the most important thing of all.

God gave us the Ten Commandments to obey. But He also gave us something even greater. Because God loves us and He wants us to live with Him in Heaven, He sent His only Son, Jesus Christ to earth. Jesus never sinned. But He died on the cross to take the punishment for all of our sins. God made the way to Heaven very simple. All you have to do is believe that Jesus is God's Son and that He died on the cross for your sins. Then, pray and ask Jesus to come live inside your heart. Ask Him to forgive you and then turn away from your sins. That's all there is to it... Jesus is waiting for you to ask Him into your heart.

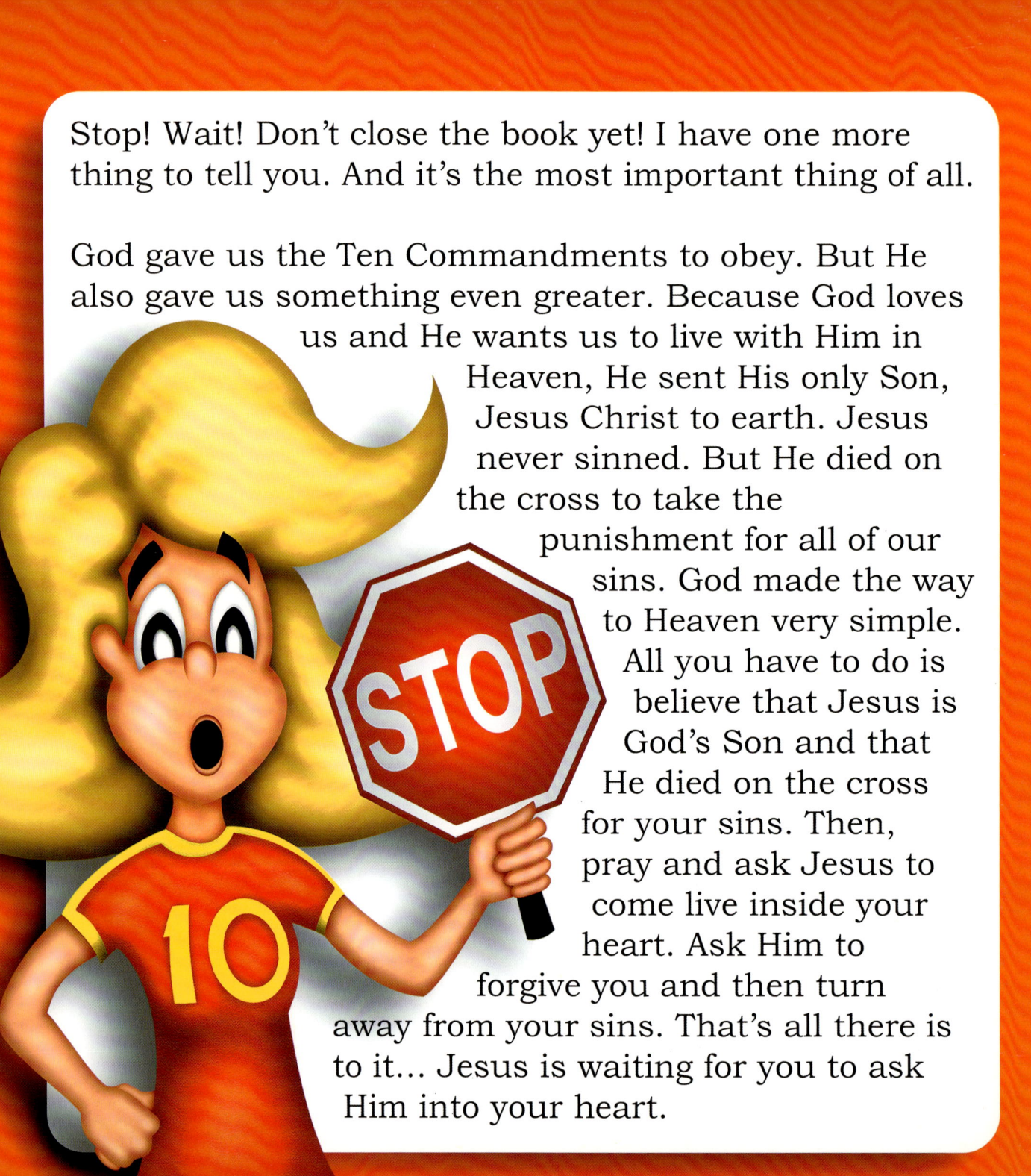

For God so loved the world, that He gave His only begotten Son, that whosoever believeth in Him should not perish, but have everlasting life. John 3:16

Light Bugs™ PUBLISHING

Coming Soon from Light Bugs Publishing!

SAMSON AND DELILAH

Join Sally for another Bible adventure as she narrates the life and times of the wild-haired Israelite hero.

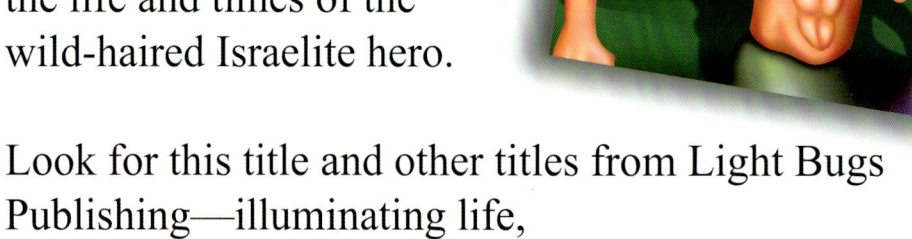

Look for this title and other titles from Light Bugs Publishing—illuminating life, adventure, fun times, and Bible stories.

Visit us at www.lightbugspublishing.com or call 850.291.7017